JAZZ VOCAL SOLOS

MW01179011

With Combo Accompaniment

Arranged by DAVE WOLPE

A Collection of 10 Songs Featuring Vocal Soloist

WB MUSIC JAZZ

B♭ Tenor Saxophone

Contents

INSTRUMENTATION

- Solo Vocalist (SPVM03001)
- B♭ Trumpet (SPVM03002)
- E♭ Alto Saxophone (SPVM03003)
- B♭ Tenor Saxophone (SPVM03004)
- Trombone (SPVM03005)
- Guitar (SPVM03006)
- Bass (SPVM03007)
- Drums (SPVM03008)
- Piano/Conductor (SPVM03009)

Project Manager: **Pete BarenBregge**
Production Coordinator: **Edmond Randle**
Design & Art Layout: **Lisa Greene Mane**

NICE WORK IF YOU CAN GET IT

B♭ TENOR SAXOPHONE

Music and Lyrics by
GEORGE GERSHWIN and IRA GERSHWIN
Arranged by DAVE WOLPE

33
mf
TO CODA
42
SOLO
F#MI7 G9
F#MI7 BMI7
EMI7 EMI7/A
D
50
SOLO
D Db7(#5)
C13 B9
EMI7 EMI7/A
D
D.S. 𝄋 AL CODA
CODA
f
mf
mf

EMBRACEABLE YOU

B♭ TENOR SAXOPHONE

Music and Lyrics by
GEORGE GERSHWIN and IRA GERSHWIN
Arranged by DAVE WOLPE

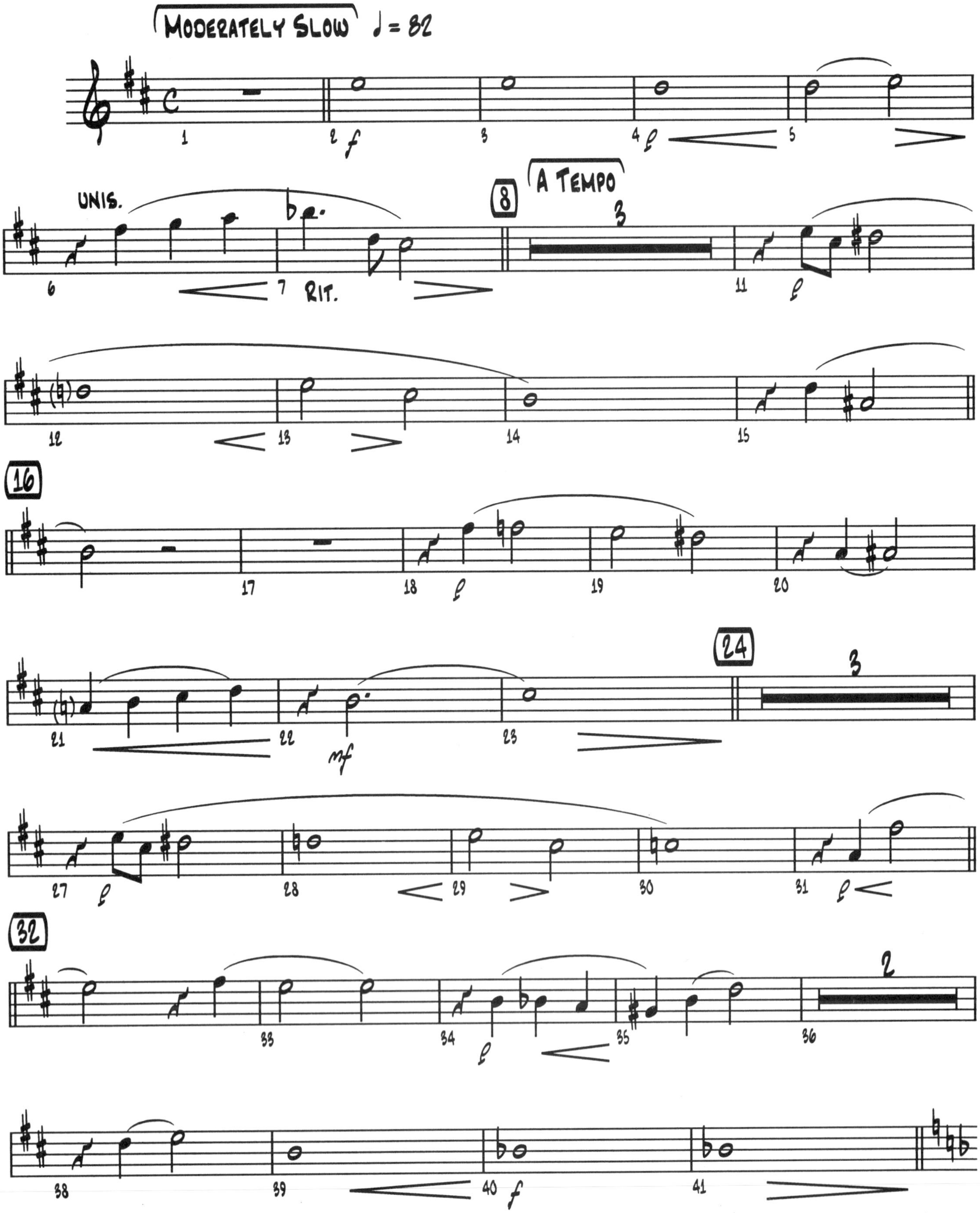

42
50
58
66
74
A TEMPO
RIT.
RIT.

LOVE IS HERE TO STAY

B♭ TENOR SAXOPHONE

Music and Lyrics by
GEORGE GERSHWIN and IRA GERSHWIN
Arranged by DAVE WOLPE

35
TO CODA
3
43
51
SOLO
A7
DMI7 G7
CMAJ7 FMAJ7
BMI7 E7 (b9)
AMI7
D9
DMI7
G9
D.S. % AL CODA
CODA
mf
fp
f

THE MAN I LOVE

Bb TENOR SAXOPHONE

Music and Lyrics by
GEORGE GERSHWIN and IRA GERSHWIN
Arranged by DAVE WOLPE

37
LEAD
NO LEAD
53
61
RIT.

YOU DO SOMETHING TO ME

B♭ TENOR SAXOPHONE

Words and Music by
COLE PORTER
Arranged By DAVE WOLPE

43
SOLO
CMAJ7
C6
C#o
DMI7
G7
DMI7
EMI7
A9
DMI7
A9
D9
AMI7
D7
DMI7
G13
G7(#5 b9)
59
UNIS.
67
D.S. % AL CODA
CODA

DO NOTHIN' TILL YOU HEAR FROM ME

B♭ Tenor Saxophone

Music by DUKE ELLINGTON
Lyric by BOB RUSSELL
Arranged by DAVE WOLPE

Solo
38
D
Bmi7 Bbmi7
Ami7
D13
Gmaj9
C13
D
B7(#5 b9)
Emi9
A13
D
F13(#11)
Emi9
46
Bbo(add E)
Ami7
D7(#5 b9)
Gmaj9
C13
D
B7(#5 b9)
Emi9
A13
D
C13
D6/9
54
62
Molto Rit.

THE LADY IS A TRAMP

B♭ TENOR SAXOPHONE

Words by LORENZ HART
Music by RICHARD RODGERS
Arranged by DAVE WOLPE

43
61
69
1.
2.
f
p

HOW LONG HAS THIS BEEN GOING ON?

Bb TENOR SAXOPHONE

Music and Lyrics by
GEORGE GERSHWIN and IRA GERSHWIN
Arranged by DAVE WOLPE

37
SOLO
D/F#
Bb7/F
EMI7
B7(#5 b9)
E9
A7(#5)
A13
F#MI7
45
SOLO
AMI7
D9
GMAJ7
C13
D/F#
Bb7/F
EMI7
B7(#5 b9)
E9
Bb9
A9
D
BMI7
AMI7
D7
53
GMAJ7
61
RUBATO
A TEMPO
(SOLO FILL)
E7(#9)
RIT.

SUMMERTIME

(From PORGY AND BESS®)

By GEORGE GERSHWIN,
DuBOSE and DOROTHY HEYWARD
and IRA GERSHWIN
Arranged by DAVE WOLPE

B♭ TENOR SAXOPHONE

33
43
2
4
61
CRESC.
69
RIT.

MOONLIGHT IN VERMONT

Bb Tenor Saxophone

Music by KARL SUESSDORF
Lyric by JOHN BLACKBURN
Arranged by DAVE WOLPE

DMI7
DMI7/G
C(9)
48
56
66
1.
2.
73
UNIS. W/VOCAL
81
mf